VISITS
to the
MOST BLESSED
SACRAMENT
and the
BLESSED
VIRGIN MARY

St. Alphonsus Liguori

A Redemptorist Pastoral Publication

Liguori

Imprimi Potest:
Edmund T. Langton, CSsR
Provincial, St. Louis Province
The Redemptorists

Imprimatur:
+ Joseph Elmer Ritter
Archbishop, Archdiocese of St. Louis

ISBN 978-0-89243-770-2
Library of Congress Catalog Card Number: 94-78485

Liguori Publications, a nonprofit corporation, is an apostolate
of the Redemptorists. To learn more about the Redemptorists,
visit Redemptorists.com.

Design: Pam Hummelsheim

Printed in the United States of America
18 19 20 21 22 / 16 15 14 13 12

FOREWORD

Saint Alphonsus de Liguori, the founder of the Redemptorist Congregation, wrote these *Visits* in the year 1745. Their publication was like casting fire upon the earth, which immediately inflamed divine love in the hearts of humanity.

Since that time these *Visits* have been translated into many languages. This present edition is a *thought translation* of the original Italian. No radical changes have been made. Variations appear in the word order and sentence structure. Unnecessary repetition and irrelevant examples have been eliminated. The translator's purpose has been to transpose the genius of the Italian language into the American idiom. It is hoped that his effort will enhance the fervor of present lovers of our Lord in the Blessed Sacrament and increase the number of those who visit him lovingly each day.

Christopher Farrell, CSsR
Liguori Publications, Book Department

INTRODUCTORY PRAYER

To be said before each Visit

My Lord Jesus Christ, I believe that you are really here in this sacrament. Night and day you remain here compassionate and loving. You call, you wait for, you welcome, everyone who comes to visit you.

Unimportant though I am, I adore you. I thank you for all the wonderful graces you have given me. But I thank you especially for having given me yourself in this sacrament, for having asked your own Mother to mother me, for having called me here to talk to you.

I am here before you today to do three things: to thank you for these precious gifts, to make up for all the disrespect that you receive in this sacrament from those who offend you, to adore you everywhere in the world where you are present in this living bread but are left abandoned and unloved.

My Jesus, I love you with all my heart. I know I have displeased you often in the past—I am sorry. With your help I promise never to do it again. I am only a miserable sinner, but I consecrate myself to you completely. I give you my will, my love, my desires, everything I own. From now on do what you please with me. All I ask is that you love me, that you keep me faithful to the end of my life. I ask for the grace to do your will exactly as you want it done.

I pray for the souls in purgatory—especially for those who were close to you in this sacrament and close to your Mother Mary. I pray for every soul hardened in sin. My Savior, I unite my love to the love of your divine heart, and I offer them both together to your Father. I beg him to accept this offering in your name. Amen.

SPIRITUAL COMMUNION

To be said before each Visit

My Jesus, I believe you are really here in the Blessed Sacrament. I love you more than anything in the world, and I hunger to feed on your flesh. But since I cannot receive Communion at this moment, feed my soul at least spiritually. I unite myself to you now as I do when I actually receive you. Never let me drift away from you.

CONCLUDING PRAYER

To be said each day

Most Holy Immaculate Virgin and my Mother Mary, to you who are the Mother of my Lord, the Queen of the world, the Advocate, the Hope, the Refuge of sinners, I have recourse today—I, who am the most miserable of all. I render you my most humble homage, O great Queen, and I thank you for all the graces you have conferred on me until now, particularly for having delivered me from hell, which I have so often deserved. I love you, O most amiable Lady; and for the love which I bear you, I promise to serve you always and to do all in my power to make others also love you. I place in you all my hopes; I confide my salvation to your care. Accept me for your servant and receive me under your mantle, O Mother of Mercy. And since you are so powerful with God, deliver me from all temptations, or rather obtain for me the strength to triumph over them until death. Of you I ask a perfect love for Jesus Christ. From you I hope to die a good death. O my Mother, by the love which you bear to God, I beseech you to help me at all times, but especially at the last moment of my life. Leave me not, I beseech you, until you see me safe in heaven, blessing you and singing your mercies for all eternity.

Amen. So I hope. So may it be.

FIRST VISIT ✓

Introductory Prayer, page 5

You are kneeling before a fountain. From its calm depths a voice whispers: *If you are thirsty, come to me.* It is Christ in the Blessed Sacrament. From this fountain of love he pours out upon the world all the merits of his sufferings. From it the saints drink deeply. The prophet predicted it: *You shall drink with joy from the Savior's fountain.*

A Spanish Poor Clare loved to make long visits to the Blessed Sacrament. The other nuns asked what she did during those long silent hours. "I could kneel there forever," she answered. "And why not? God is there. You wonder what I do in the presence of my God? I marvel, I love, I thank, I beg. What does a tramp do when he meets a millionaire? A sick man when he sees a doctor? A starving man when he sees food? What does a dry-throated hiker do at a drinking fountain?"

My Jesus: You are my Life, my Hope, my Treasure, my soul's only Love. A cruel death was the price you paid to be here in this sacrament today. And even now you suffer insults from those who ignore you. Yet, you remain because you want our love.

Come, my Lord, implant yourself in my heart. Lock its door forever. I want nothing cheap to enter it and take away the love that belongs to you. You alone must run my life. If I swerve from you, steer me straight once more. Make me search for one pleasure: the pleasure of pleasing you. Make me yearn for one joy: the joy of visiting you. Make me crave for one delight: the delight of receiving your body. So many people chase after such hollow things! But all I care about is your love, and I am here to beg it from you today. Let me forget myself and keep you ever before my mind. Amen.

Spiritual Communion, page 6

Visit With Mary

We have another fountain to drink from too...our Mother Mary. Saint Bernard said that Mary is so rich in graces that everybody shares in them: "Of her fullness we have all received." Mary was literally filled with grace, as the angel said when he greeted her. God filled her with such tremendous riches so that she could share them with her children. Cause of our joy, pray for us!

Concluding Prayer, page 7

SECOND VISIT

Introductory Prayer, page 5

An old priest once expressed this beautiful thought: Bread is a food that will keep when preserved. That is why Christ chose to remain in the world under the form of bread—not only to feed his lovers in holy Communion but also to be preserved in the tabernacle. There he would stay with us always. There we would have an ever-present reminder of his love.

Saint Paul is astounded to see Jesus take on *the form of a slave.* But what should we say when we see him take on the form of bread? Saint Peter Alcantara said that words can give no idea of the love Jesus has for souls that are his friends. To make sure these souls would not forget him, he has chosen to live near them in this sacrament. He wants nothing to come between him and his faithful friends.

My Jesus, you are here in the tabernacle precisely to listen to those who come to tell you their troubles and to ask you for help. I beg you to listen to this ungrateful sinner. My heart is heavy as I kneel here before you. Heavy because I see how much I have displeased you. I have stung your heart with my sins. Will you forgive and forget everything?

There is something else too. I have seen how good and kind you are and I have fallen in love with you. I want to love you, to please you. But I am a weakling; I need help. O great Lord, show heaven your power! Change my selfishness into genuine love. I know you can do it, I know you want to do it. Give me the means to love you with all my heart. At least let my love be as selfless as my sins have been selfish. My Jesus, I love you more than anything else in the world. I love you even more than my own life.

Spiritual Communion, page 6

Visit With Mary

Let us confidently approach God's throne, the source of grace, to obtain mercy and find grace to help us when we need it. Saint Antoninus used to say that the throne from which God dispenses all his graces is Mary. My Queen, I know you want to help sinners. Look at me: I am a miserable sinner who turns to you. Refuge of sinners, please help me!

Concluding Prayer, page 7

THIRD VISIT

Introductory Prayer, page 5

I am delighted to be with humanity. These are the words of our God. Dying for us was not enough for him. He wanted to remain with us in this Blessed Sacrament. "O men," moans Saint Teresa, "how can you offend a God who says that he is delighted to be with you?" He is highly pleased to be with us. Should we not find comfort and peace in being with him? Let us thank him for loving us and talk to him heart to heart.

Here I am, Lord, kneeling before this altar where you remain a "shut-in" for me night and day. You are the

Fountain of grace, the Healer of the sick, the Helper of the helpless. Have mercy on a sick and helpless sinner. But I will not let my sad condition discourage me because I know that you are in this living bread to help me. I adore you! I thank you! I love you! Please listen as I plead with you: Give me the courage and the strength to love you.

Lord, I love you from the depths of my soul. I love you with all the love I own. Help me to put meaning into those words. Mary, my Mother, my patron saints, angels in heaven, help me to love my God.

Spiritual Communion, page 6

Visit With Mary

Her chains are saving chains. A certain holy man said that devotion to Mary is like a chain that pulls us up to heaven. Let us ask our Lady to keep drawing us to herself by that chain of trust and love, O kind, O loving, O sweet Virgin Mary!

Concluding Prayer, page 7

FOURTH VISIT

Introductory Prayer, page 5

Real friends want to be with one another every moment they can spare. Sometimes they spend entire days together. Christ's friends are that way too; kneeling before the Blessed Sacrament is the great joy of their life. They have found that *his talk is not bitter, his company not boring.* But those who do not love Christ become bored in his presence.

From heaven Saint Teresa appeared to one of her Carmelite nuns. She told her that souls in heaven and souls in the world should really love God with the same love. "The only difference," she said, "is that we love God face to face; you must love him in the Blessed Sacrament." Yes, this living bread is our heaven on earth.

My Savior, you rescued me from my sins by your painful death on the cross. You paid for me in blood, and you keep fresh that sacrifice in every Mass. Do not let all this love go to waste: Never let me slip away from you. I put myself at your service. Use me as you please. I give you my will so that you can chain it to yours. I want to be your slave. No longer will I live to please myself, but only to satisfy you. Detach from my soul whatever displeases you. Let me live with the single thought of pleasing you.

My God, I love you with all my heart because you desire it and you deserve it. I only wish I could love you as you really deserve. O Lord, make my wish come true! Give me your love!

Spiritual Communion, page 6

Visit With Mary

I am the Mother of gracious love. These words of holy Scripture are applied to Mary whose love makes souls so beautiful. A saint used to think of Mary as a gentle Mother who gave away the sweet liquid of divine love. Only Mary gives this sweet liquid. Let us ask our gentle Mother for it. O my Mother, help me to give myself completely to Jesus.

Concluding Prayer, page 7

FIFTH VISIT

Introductory Prayer, page 5

In the Psalms we read: *The sparrow finds a home, and the swallow a nest for her young: your altars, my King and my God.* Like the birds of the air, my Love, you too have made a nest—a home upon our altars. There we can always find you. There you are forever our companion.

Lord, you love us too much. There is nothing more you can do to make us love you. How unreasonable we are if our love is cool and distant. Give us the strength to love you intensely! Draw us gently to your love. Make us see the great claim you have on our affection.

O infinite God, what have you not done to win the hearts of humanity? Why do so few love you in return? I am one of those ungrateful ones. But no more. I resolve to love you and to let nothing come between us again. You deserve my love and you urge me to give it to you. Let me satisfy you to the full. My hope is in the riches of your passion. Give all the wealth in the world to people who ask you for it. I am interested only in the tremendous treasure of your love.

I love you, my Jesus. You alone are my Treasure; you alone can satisfy me; you alone are my Love. You have spent yourself lavishly for me. Now I must live my life for you.

Spiritual Communion, page 6

Visit With Mary

My Lady, Saint Bernard says that you ravish hearts, that you steal them by your sweetness and kindness. Take my heart, too, my Queen—I give it to you. Lay it before God with your own. Mother of love, pray for me!

Concluding Prayer, page 7

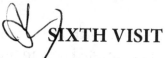

SIXTH VISIT

Introductory Prayer, page 5

Where your treasure is, there too your heart is bound to be. Christ says that a person's affections converge on the spot where one believes the treasure to lie. Saints have Christ as their only treasure, and their affections are all centered on the Blessed Sacrament.

O hidden Christ, you remain night and day in your tabernacle-prison with undying love! Rouse my sluggish heart. Make it think of you, love you, search for you, trust in you alone. Do this through the power of your sufferings; they are my hope.

My divine Lover, your devices to attract souls are truly amazing. Dying for us did not satisfy you. You had to give us this sacrament as a companion, as food, as a pledge of heaven. You had to become a tiny baby, a poor laborer, a beaten criminal, even a morsel of bread. Only a God who loves us deeply could conceive such ideas!

But when am I going to respond to your insistent love? Lord, I want to live to love you. My life is worthless if I do not use it for that. And what is there to love but you, who are so good, so kind, so lovable? May my soul expand with love when it thinks of you. And when it hears the names crib, cross, sacrament, may it be sparked with the desire to do great things for you. O Lord, let me do something for you before I die!

Spiritual Communion, page 6

Visit With Mary

Mary has been compared to *the olive tree* of holy Scripture that gives oil—the oil of mercy. And she reveals herself openly so that everyone can obtain this soothing oil from her. Let us pray with Saint Bernard: "Remember, my Mother, it is unheard of that anyone trusting in your help has ever been abandoned." O holy Queen, I know that you will not abandon me. Give me the grace to call on you always.

Concluding Prayer, page 7

♫SEVENTH VISIT

Introductory Prayer, page 5

I am with you at all times, as long as the world will last. Our loving Shepherd gave his life for us, his sheep. But he would not let even death sever himself from us. "Here I am, my sheep," he says. "I have remained on earth in this sacrament to shepherd you through every day of your lives. Here you can run to me whenever you need help and a word of comfort. I will not leave you until time comes to an end, until your days on earth are done."

Saint Peter Alcantara used another comparison: "The Bridegroom would not have his bride lonely while he was away. He wanted her to have a companion. And the best companion he could leave her was himself in this sacrament."

My lovable Savior, I have come to visit you to show my love. But when you visit my soul in holy Communion, you bring a love far greater than mine! Not only do you visit me, you become my food; you become one with me. At that thrilling moment I can truthfully whisper: "Now, my Jesus, you are all mine." You offer yourself completely to me; it is only reasonable that I make a gift of myself to you. But I am nothing...you are God! When, O God of love, will my actions begin to speak louder than my words? You can make it happen. Deepen my trust in you by the merits of your blood. Then, before death calls, perhaps I will belong entirely to you and no longer to myself.

My Lord, not a single prayer escapes you. Listen to the plea of a soul who is thirsting to love you. I want to love you with all my strength. I want to obey your every wish without self-interest, consolation, reward. I want to serve only to love, only to satisfy, only to please your loving heart. Loving you will be reward enough. Take my freedom, take my will, take everything I own, take my whole being...but give me yourself. I love you, I long for you, I hunger for you, I yearn for you! O my Jesus, make me all your own.

Spiritual Communion, page 6

Visit With Mary

O loving Lady, we call you our hope. You are the hope of all; be mine also. "The whole reason for my hope," Saint Bernard called you. He urges those about to despair to put their trust in you. My Mother, do not let me give in to despair. I place my trust in you. O Mother of God, pray to Jesus for me.

Concluding Prayer, page 7

EIGHTH VISIT

Introductory Prayer, page 5

To every soul that visits the Blessed Sacrament, Christ in the words of the spouse in the Song of Songs says: *Rise. Hurry, my friend! Come, my beautiful one. Rise* above your troubles. I am here to enrich you with grace. *Hurry* to my side. Do not fear my majesty; it is hidden in this bread to overcome your fear and to give you confidence. *My friend,* you are no longer my enemy, for you love me and I love you. *My beautiful one,* God's grace fills you with splendor. *Come,* throw yourself into my arms; tell me your every wish without fear.

Saint Teresa said that the King of Glory disguised himself in this bread of life to encourage us to approach his heart with bold confidence. Let us then go to him with boundless trust and love. Let us ask for his powerful graces.

A God-Man present in this sacrament for me! What a comfort! What a privilege to know that I kneel before God! And to think that this God *loves* me! Lovers of God, wherever you are, love him for me too. Mary, my Mother, help me to love him. And you, my lovable Lord, become the goal of my heart's desires. Become the sole owner of my will. Possess me completely. I offer you my mind; may it think only of how good you are. I offer you my body; may it always please you. I offer you my soul; may it be yours forever.

O divine Lover, I wish all men knew how tenderly you love each one of them. Then surely they would worship you and live to please you, as you desire and deserve. Let me at least live only to love you. From this moment I will begin to do everything I can to satisfy you. I resolve to cast aside anything that displeases you. No price is too high…not even my life. What a blessing it would be to lose everything to gain you…my God, my Treasure, my Love, my Everything!

Spiritual Communion, page 6

Visit With Mary

Let all little ones come to me. Mary calls all children who need a mother. She wants them to run to her, the most loving Mother there is. A mother's love for her children is well known. Try to imagine the depth of Mary's love for her spiritual children! Mother of my soul, no one outside of God desires my salvation more than you do. Show me that you are really my mother.

Concluding Prayer, page 7

NINTH VISIT

Introductory Prayer, page 5

A certain holy priest liked to think of Christ in the Blessed Sacrament with his arms loaded with graces, waiting to give them away. Here I am, Lord, ready to receive them.

My God, I realize that you deserve to be loved more than anything else in the world. I want to love you as profoundly as the human heart can love. But, traitor and rebel that I am, I am not entitled to this love. I am not worthy to kneel here before you. Yet you ask us to love: *My sons and daughters, give me your hearts.* You command us: *Love the Lord with all your heart.* I really believe this is why you have spared my life: to give me another chance to love you.

Since this is the way you want it, Lord, I yield to your request and command. I offer myself to you; I love you. Only you can cultivate my barren heart. It is a cold, cramped, calloused heart; but since you ask for it, it is yours. Surely if you accept it, you will rid it of all selfishness.

Change me, Lord! By ignoring you, I have been extremely ungrateful. I haven't the nerve to ignore you any longer. Your boundless goodness deserves boundless love. Starting right now, let me make up for all the love I have held back in the past. My God, I am really serious about wanting to love you.

Spiritual Communion, page 6

Visit With Mary

Mary is like Jesus in many ways. Because she is the Mother of Mercy, she is glad to help and comfort stumbling sinners. In fact, she is so eager to fill souls with choice graces that a holy man once said: "This Mother is more anxious to help us with her graces than we are anxious to receive them." O Mary, you are our hope!

Concluding Prayer, page 7

TENTH VISIT

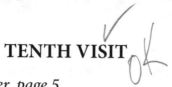

Introductory Prayer, page 5

"People are foolish," says Saint Augustine, "when they seek satisfaction in worldly things." He urges them to come to Christ who alone can satisfy the craving of their hearts. My soul, don't be a fool; yearn only for God. It is easy to find him, for he is close by in the tabernacle. Tell him your needs. He is here precisely to comfort you and listen to you.

Not just anybody is allowed to talk to an important person, says Saint Teresa. Perhaps the closest contact will be through a secretary. But there are no go-betweens when we talk to you, my Lord. In this sacrament you do not stand on your dignity; you are never too busy for anyone. We need only present our problems to find a ready Listener. And even if a person finally does get an interview with an important person, how much red tape is involved! Busy people are stingy with their time. But you receive us night and day at our convenience.

O divine Lover, you are an expert at stealing hearts with your love. They fall in love with you; they are astonished at your tenderness; they cannot turn their thoughts away from you. Steal my heart too. It wants to love you humbly. From this day forward I put my interests, my hopes, my love, my soul, my body—everything—in your hands.

Accept me, Lord, and do what you please with me. Never again will I complain about the way you run my life. I know that your loving heart is shaping every hour for my welfare. All I need to know is that your will is involved. At once I shall make my desires harmonize with yours. Treat me as you please. I submit my will entirely to your will—a will so good, so gentle, so lovable. Your will is precious to me. I want to live and die its prisoner. Your pleasure is my pleasure; your desires are my desires.

My God, give me the courage to live for you alone, to love what you love. Let me die for you as you died for me. I deeply regret the times I have so selfishly ignored you. O will of God, I love you because you are one with God. I put myself at your command. You are my Love!

Spiritual Communion, page 6

Visit With Mary

The words of holy Scripture, *I have riches…to give to those who love me,* have been applied to Mary. If we want these riches of grace, we must love her. A holy man named her "the Treasurer of Grace." Happy is the man who goes to this Treasurer with confidence and love. My Mother and my hope, you can make me a saint! I depend on you for this grace.

Concluding Prayer, page 7

ELEVENTH VISIT

Introductory Prayer, page 5

"Never wander from Christ the loving Shepherd," advises Saint Teresa. "The sheep that press close to the shepherd are always stroked more lovingly and fed morsels of his own food. If the shepherd dozes off, the lamb will not wander. It waits till he wakens to receive a new gift for its loyalty."

My Redeemer-Shepherd, here I am close to you in this sacrament. The only gift I want is a burning and lasting love for you. Thank you, my faith, for assuring me that what looks like bread in the tabernacle is really my Lord Jesus Christ. And that he is there because he loves me! My Lord, my Everything, I believe you are really present in this sacrament. You are hidden from my human eyes. But with the eyes of my faith I see in the host the King of heaven and earth, the world's loving Savior.

My Jesus, you are my Hope, my Salvation, my Strength, my Joy. I want you to be my Love: the only one I think about, the only one I desire, the only one I adore. I rejoice when I realize that you are happy beyond measure and shall always be so. This thought alone gives me more pleasure than anything I could ever experience.

Take charge of my soul, Lord. I lay it before you and beg you to become Master of it forever. I want my will, my senses, and my talents to be subject to your love. I want to use them only to give you pleasure and glory.

Spiritual Communion, page 6

Visit With Mary

Happy is the man who watches at my gate and waits at my doorstep. The poor man begs for a gift at the rich man's gate. That was your life, sweet Mother of Jesus. Help me, teach me to live like you did: happy because you belonged to God. My Hope, help me!

Concluding Prayer, page 7

TWELFTH VISIT

Introductory Prayer, page 5

God is love. The man who lives in love lives in God, and God lives in him. The lover of Christ, too, lives in Christ and Christ in him: *Anyone who loves me will win my Father's love....We will come and make our home in him.*

When Saint Philip Neri received holy Communion on his deathbed, the old saint gasped, "Here is my Love!" Let us repeat these words to Christ present before us: "Here is my Love...here is the goal of my love for life, for eternity!"

My Lord and my God, you promised that you will love those who love you. That you will even come and make your home within them forever. I love you, Lord. I love you more than anything in the world. Love me in return. I beg you because I value your love more than all the world's treasures. Come, make your home in my soul. Plant yourself firmly so that you will never have to leave. Or better, so that I will never again evict you from your home within me. You will not leave unless rejected. I rejected you before, and I may do it again. What a crime!

What senseless ingratitude! You treat me as your favorite, and I scorn your love! But this might happen again. I would rather die, because if I die your friend, I will live united with you forever.

This is what I live for, my Jesus. Make me love you always. I know you will always love me in return. May our friendship never end!

Spiritual Communion, page 6

Visit With Mary

Many phrases of the Old Testament have been referred to Mary. *Those who are dedicated to my cause shall not sin.* Those who pray to her will persevere to the end. Those who make her known and loved by others are well on their way to heaven. I promise that I will broadcast your glories in public and in private. O holy Virgin, make me worthy to sing your praises.

Concluding Prayer, page 7

THIRTEENTH VISIT

Introductory Prayer, page 5

My eyes and my heart will be there always. Christ in the Blessed Sacrament is witness to this promise. He is with us night and day. Surely it would have been enough, Lord, to remain in the tabernacle during the day only. Then your lovers would find it easier to keep you company. But why remain all through the night? When darkness comes, churches close, people go home, and you are left all alone.

I think I understand: *Love* has made you our prisoner. Your extravagant love has entombed you in this tabernacle-prison. Night and day it prevents you from leaving. Such intense love should compel us to keep you company until we are forced to say good-bye. Even then we should leave our hearts at your feet. For here is a God all alone in a tabernacle; who is "all eyes" to provide for our needs; "all heart" to love us; a God who eagerly awaits our return with the dawn of each new day.

My Jesus, I want to please you. I give you my will, I give you my love. You are in this sacrament not only to be near us but also to feed us. Uninvited, I would not dare to receive you in Communion. But since you urge me so strongly, how can I dare stay away? You are here in this sacrament to become food for our souls and master of our hearts. To be lovingly united with us is your chief concern.

Come, my Jesus, come! I desire to receive you within my heart to become the Ruler of my will. I yield everything within me to your love: my delights, my pleasures, my freedom. Lead me, conquer me, rid me completely of whatever is mine and not yours. Let my soul feed on you in holy Communion. Never let it be captivated by creatures that will hold it back from you. I love you alone, my God, and I want to love you forever. Lead me toward you with the chains of love.

Spiritual Communion, page 6

Visit With Mary

"Seek for grace through Mary," Saint Bernard urges us. She is the Treasurer of Grace. She can and will enrich us with grace. She even invites us: "Let those who are little ones come to me." O lovable Lady, gracious and gentle, please look after me—a timid soul who trusts you completely. O Mother of God, we run to you for help!

Concluding Prayer, page 7

FOURTEENTH VISIT

Introductory Prayer, page 5

Jesus, from your tabernacle you fulfill the words of the psalmist: *This is my resting place forever; here have I chosen to live.* You want to live near us in this sacrament. You find rest here because you love us. Then it is only reasonable that we should want to live near you always—at least in desire—and that we should find peace and rest in your presence. Loving souls, you are fortunate to be enjoying the soothing rest that comes from being close to Christ. I, too, would be fortunate, Lord, if I would find nothing more delightful than being in your presence.

Why have I wasted so many years without loving you? I deeply regret those lost years! But I praise the boundless patience that has put up with me for so long. I have been so selfish, and still you wait for me! Why? So that your mercy and love might attract me and make me yours completely.

My Lord, I can no longer resist the power of your love. I offer you the rest of my life. I expect you to help me keep faithful to my promise. You loved me even when I turned my back on you. Surely now that I yearn for you, you will favor me with rich graces. Give me the grace to love you, my God! I love you with all my heart, more than anything in the world, more than my life. I am ashamed of my sins—forgive me. Inflame my heart with love…a love that will last till I die and endure through eternity.

All-powerful God, show the world your might: Make me one of your most ardent lovers! Do it through your merits, my Jesus. This is my desire, my resolve for life.

You have inspired me with your love; give me the courage to never stop loving you. I thank you for having been so patient with me until now.

Spiritual Communion, page 6

Visit With Mary

A certain saint used to say to Mary: "No one can be saved without you; no one can be freed from sin without you; no one receives graces without you." Well then, my Lady, if you do not help me, I am lost. And if lost, I could never love you in heaven. However, you never abandon those who ask for help. Only those who do not ask are lost. So, I turn to you and place all my trust in you. You are the reason for my hope.

Concluding Prayer, page 7

FIFTEENTH VISIT

Introductory Prayer, page 5

To cast fire upon the earth—that is my mission! And how I wish it were already burning fiercely! Nothing in the world can set hearts ablaze with love for God like the Blessed Sacrament. That is why this divine bread has been pictured as a furnace of love. Saint Catherine of Siena saw far-reaching flames coming from this furnace of love and spreading throughout the world. Seeing this, Catherine simply could not understand how so many people could live without loving God.

My Lord, set me on fire with love for you. Let me think of nothing, crave for nothing, yearn for nothing, search for nothing, but you. How I wish to be caught up in this scorching fire of love! How I wish it would consume every obstacle that blocks my path toward you! Make my love for you grow stronger each day of my life.

My Jesus, for me you become a victim of love in each Eucharistic sacrifice. It is only reasonable that I make a gift of myself to you. My Father, I offer you my soul, my will, my life. I unite this small human sacrifice to the tremendous divine sacrifice of your Son: his actual death on the cross and its mystical renewal in each sacrifice on our altars. Unite my sacrifice with his.

Give me the grace to live up to my offering, Lord, every day of my life. Let me die sacrificing myself for your cause. I would love to die a martyr's death. But if I do not deserve such a privilege, let me at least offer you my life, and let me accept my death willingly. I really desire this grace,

Lord. In my dying moments I want to accept your will completely—to honor and please you. As of now I offer you my death, whenever and wherever it arrives. My Jesus, I want my death to please you.

Spiritual Communion, page 6

Visit With Mary

My Queen, let me call you what Saint Bernard calls you: "The reason for my hope." I join Saint Damascene in saying: "I have placed all my hopes in you." Inspire me to seek forgiveness of my sins and perseverance until death.

You are the channel of God's saving graces. You must save me too! Will my salvation, dear Lady. You see to the salvation of everyone who perseveres in praying to you. Here I am, then, begging for that grace.

Concluding Prayer, page 7

SIXTEENTH VISIT

Introductory Prayer, page 5

Millions of souls would be freed from their misery if they would only come to this living bread. Here alone will they find the medicine that can cure their spiritual sickness. We hear the prophet Jeremiah groan: *Is there no medicine, no doctor in Gilead?* This Gilead is a mountain in Arabia, famous for its healing herbs. One writer calls it a symbol of Christ in the Blessed Sacrament. For, greater than Gilead, this sacrament has every cure for our troubled spirits.

"Why do you complain when something goes wrong?" our Redeemer could very well ask us. "Here in this sacrament you have the doctor and the medicine that can heal every soul. *Come to me, and I will refresh you.*" Let us answer with the sisters of Lazarus: *Lord, your friend is sick.* I am that sick friend, Lord. My soul bleeds from the wounds of its many sins. Divine Doctor, I come to you to be healed. You can cure me: *Heal my soul, Lord, for it has sinned against you.*

Lead me to you by the great drawing power of your love. I would rather be your servant than master of the whole world. Your love is all I want from life. What I have I give you, Lord. But even if the whole universe were mine, I would give that up in favor of you. Still I renounce what I can: relatives, comforts, pleasures, freedom, even spiritual consolations. I want to give you all my love. I love you more than myself, and I hope to love you forever in eternity. My Jesus, I offer myself to you; accept me!

Spiritual Communion, page 6

Visit With Mary

"No matter how many sins a man has committed, if he comes to me with a desire to change his life, I welcome him. I am more interested in the sincerity of his desire than in the hatefulness of his sins. I am always ready to soothe and heal the gaping wounds of his soul. That is why my name is 'Mother of Mercy.'"

These are the words you spoke to Saint Bridget, my Lady. You can heal me, and you want to heal me. Here I stand, Doctor of Souls. Heal the cuts and bruises of sin that mark my soul. A single whispered word to your Son will heal me. Have pity on me, great Queen!

Concluding Prayer, page 7

SEVENTEENTH VISIT

Introductory Prayer, page 5

Lovers long to be in the company of each other. Here we are in the company of Christ, our Lover. He sees us and hears us. Have we nothing to say to him? Let us enjoy his presence and be glad that he is receiving glory and love in the Blessed Sacrament from many souls. Would that every person in the world offered him his heart! At least let us offer him our own genuine love. He should be our only love, our only desire.

A holy priest named Salesius felt deep joy merely in speaking about the Blessed Sacrament. His thirst for visiting his divine Lover was never quenched. He used every chance he could to drop in for a visit: before answering parlor calls, on going to his room, while walking the corridors of the monastery. Practically every hour of the day he visited our Lord on the altar. His faithful love was richly rewarded: God let him die a martyr's death while defending the Blessed Sacrament.

My Jesus, I wish I could die defending your presence in the Eucharist. You are there to prove the tenderness of your love. My Lord, since you work so many miracles in this sacrament, I beg you to work one more: Persuade me to love you alone. You desire it; you have every claim to it. Give me the courage to love you with all my heart. Give the world's treasures to anyone you please. I reject them all. Your love is all I yearn for and the only thing I beg of you. I love you, my Jesus; make me always love you. I ask nothing more.

Spiritual Communion, page 6

Visit With Mary

My Queen, how comforting is the title from your litany: "Mother most amiable." Lovable you are, my Lady. Your soul's beauty has stolen even God's heart. Saint Bonaventure said that your name alone is lovable enough to set on fire the hearts of your lovers: "O sweet, gentle, lovable Mary! The mere mention of your name inflames the heart of your lovers!"

So it is only reasonable that I love you, too, my Mother. But I do not want to be just an ordinary lover. I want to be your greatest lover after God. If my desire is bold and brash, I blame you. You have inspired it by the special favor you have shown me. If you were not so lovable, I would not desire to love you so much. Listen to my prayer, O Lady. As a sign that you have, obtain the love I seek from God. Surely he will give it, for he is pleased to see you loved. My lovable Mother, I love you beyond measure.

Concluding Prayer, page 7

EIGHTEENTH VISIT

Introductory Prayer, page 5

Christ on Judgment Day will be my all-just Judge. But in this sacrament he is my lavish Lover. If someone loves me so much that he takes up residence near me as proof of his love, to ignore him would be most ungrateful.

My Jesus, you have made your home in this sacrament because you love me. Night and day I would like to kneel at your feet. The angels never leave you because they love you so much. I, too, should try my best to please you by keeping you company, by marveling at your love and kindness. *With angels for my witnesses, I will sing your praise. I bow down in worship toward your sanctuary, to thank you for your mercy and faithfulness.*

O God, food of angels, divine nourishment, I love you. You are not satisfied with this love of mine. Nor should I be content with it. It is too irresponsible. Make me realize how good and beautiful you are! Help me to drive from my heart every worldly affection that keeps me from loving you alone. Each day you appear on the altar to prove your love and to unite yourself with me. It is only right that I think of nothing but loving, adoring, and pleasing you. I love you from the depths of my soul; I love you with all my heart. If it pleases you, reward this love of mine by making it ever deeper and stronger. Jesus, my Love, give me love!

Spiritual Communion, page 6

Visit With Mary

Penniless sick people find medical care in charity hospitals. Souls entangled in sin—though looked down on by everyone—find care and protection in Mary. God has put her in the world to be a kind of "charity hospital" for sinners. Saint Ephrem calls her "a shelter for sinners."

So, my Queen, if a sinner like me needs help, you cannot turn me away. In fact, the more sinful I am, the greater is my claim to your protection and care. That is why God created you: to be his hospital for even the most abandoned sinners. Here I am, my Mother; I put myself under your care. Be my hope of salvation. Where shall I turn if you reject me?

Concluding Prayer, page 7

NINETEENTH VISIT

Introductory Prayer, page 5

Good friends find pleasure in one another's company. Let us know pleasure in the company of our best Friend, a Friend who can do everything for us, a friend who loves us beyond measure. Here in the Blessed Sacrament we can talk to him straight from the heart. We can open our souls to him, tell him what we need, beg him for powerful graces. We are perfectly free to approach the King of the universe with full confidence and without fear.

The Old Testament tells how happy Joseph was when God descended into his dark dungeon to keep him company. How happy we should be to have God keeping us company in this dark dungeon of life. His compassionate and loving presence comforts us every hour of our day.

Poor prisoners really appreciate a friend who comes to visit them, consoles them, and raises their hope for future relief. Christ in this sacrament is that kind of friend. He assures us: *I am with you at all times.* I am here in this prison of the world precisely to console you, to help you, to rescue you. Give me a place in your life; welcome me warmly, and the problems of life will disappear. Then when it is time, I will take you home to heaven where your happiness will never end.

O God, Ocean of Love, you hide your boundless majesty under the form of bread so that you can live close to us. I resolve to visit you often. I want to enjoy your soul-soothing presence—the same presence that brings happiness to heaven's saints. I wish I could kneel here in loving adoration forever. If ever my soul grows lax in its love, if ever it becomes too involved in "getting things done," bring me back to my senses. Inflame me with a burning desire to be near you in this sacrament. If only I had always loved you! If only I had always pleased you! But I still have a chance as long as I am alive. I really want to love you, my Lord, my Treasure, my Love, my Everything. Help me to realize my desire!

Spiritual Communion, page 6

Visit With Mary

A lover of Mary used to say: "Sinner, don't give up hope! Turn to this Lady with great expectation. You will find that she can and will help you. Just think! Her desire to help you is even stronger than your desire for her help!"

I always thank God, my Lady, for having introduced me to you. To ignore you could endanger my salvation! But I love you, my Mother, and trust you so completely that I put my immortal soul into your hands. Happy is the one who trusts in you.

Concluding Prayer, page 7

OK

TWENTIETH VISIT

Introductory Prayer, page 5

Five hundred years before Christ was born, the priest-prophet Zachariah looked ahead into the coming centuries and foretold: *When that day comes, clansmen of David and citizens of Jerusalem shall have a free-flowing fountain in which the sinner will be cleansed.* This sacrament is the flowing fountain the prophet foresaw. It flows freely so that those who wish can wash away the stains of sin that spot their souls each day. For our daily faults and failings, there is no better medicine than to come to the Blessed Sacrament.

I resolve to do this always, my Lord. The waters of this fountain not only wash me but also flood my soul with light and strength to resist future falls. They brace me for suffering so that I can take it with a smile. They fill me with your love. That is why you welcome my visits: to shower me with life-changing graces.

My God, wash away every stain and every fault that I have committed today. I am sorry for having displeased you. Strengthen me against future falls by inflaming me with an intense desire to love you. I wish I could ever stay here with you, like your servant Mary Diaz used to do. She hardly ever left you! Or like a certain Carmelite who never passed a church without dropping in for a visit. He thought a person should always stop to say hello when passing near a friend's home. But a brief visit never satisfied him. He kept you company as long as he could without neglecting his duties.

My divine Lover, you have made your home in this tabernacle so that I might love you. You have given me a heart that can love profoundly. Then why don't I love you or why is my love so feeble? Your boundless goodness deserves more than a measured love. Your love for me should stir up a great fire within me. You are the Supreme Being…I am nothing. If I were to give myself completely to your service—even die for you—this would be little. But you not only sacrificed your life to redeem me, you also remain here on earth as bread to nourish me. You deserve my love, and I want you to have it. Help me to love you, my Jesus! Help me to give you what you really want from me: my heart's profoundest love.

Spiritual Communion, page 6

Visit With Mary

My loving Queen, Saint Bernard's words about you fill me with confidence. He says that you do not demand letters of recommendation; all you want to know is whether help is needed. You are ever ready to help anyone who turns to you. Then I have only to pray to you, and you will listen. Listen to me, a blundering sinner who deserves hell a thousand times. I want to change my life; I want to love the God I have offended. I make myself your slave. Save this poor sinner who now belongs to you. I hope you have understood and heard my plea. Yes, I am sure you have.

Concluding Prayer, page 7

✓TWENTY-FIRST VISIT

Introductory Prayer, page 5

It is where the body lies that the eagles will gather. Some scholars see a deeper meaning in these words: The "body" is the Body of Christ; the "eagles" are the souls who are in the world but not of it. Like soaring eagles, they fly above the things of this world. They keep their thoughts and affections pointed heavenward. These souls hover around the Blessed Sacrament as their paradise here on earth.

A certain saintly priest, no matter where he happened to be, often used to glance lovingly in the direction where he knew the tabernacle was situated. He visited his divine Lover every chance he had—sometimes all night long! Tears came to his eyes when he saw so many people standing in line to seek favors from worldly rulers and yet so few kneeling in prayer to obtain favors from the King of the universe. He considered religious to be the luckiest people in the world. They live under the same roof with God! They can visit him night and day at their convenience! No one else enjoys such privileges.

My sinfulness must make me look like a leper, Lord. Yet you speak to my soul and invite me to come closer. Undiscouraged at the sight of my sinfulness, I approach you confidently. Heal my soul! Dismiss from my heart every affection that keeps me from you, every yearning that you do not want there, every thought that is not directed toward you. My Jesus, I want to please you and to love you alone, because you alone deserve my undivided love. Detach me from everything. Then take me in your arms and hold me so closely that I will never be able to leave you either in this life or the next.

Spiritual Communion, page 6

Visit With Mary

A Carthusian monk called Mary "the defender of sinners." Great Mother of God, defending criminals who turn to you is your specialty. Here is one of them kneeling before you. I turn to you with the words of Saint Thomas Villanova: "O loving Advocate, defend my case!" I plead guilty of offending a God who has favored me with special graces. But what can I say? The harm is done. You can still save me. All you have to do is tell God you will defend my case, and I shall be forgiven and saved. My Mother, you must save me!

Concluding Prayer, page 7

TWENTY-SECOND VISIT

Introductory Prayer, page 5

The spouse in the Song of Songs searches for her lover with these words: *Have you seen him whom my soul loves?* Christ had not as yet come to live in the world. If his lovers are lonely for him now, they need only turn to the Bread of Life on the altar. A holy priest claimed that he found no place more peaceful or more restful than before a tabernacle that houses Christ.

O boundless Lover, you deserve to be boundlessly loved! To keep us company and unite yourself to our hearts, you have hidden divine dignity under the form of bread! How could you ever humble yourself so deeply? Your humility is fathomless because it matches the depths of your love.

I marvel at all the measures you have taken to captivate my love. I cannot refuse to love you. I promise that your love shall come before self-interest, self-satisfaction, self-gratification. I will find pleasure in pleasing you, my God. Make me hunger and crave to feed on your body and to keep you company continually. Only the coldest of hearts could reject the warmth of your love.

Crush every affection in me that clings to worldly things, Lord. You want my love, my desires, my affections, directed toward yourself alone. I love you, and I beg for nothing but yourself. My pleasure is to please you. Accept this desire of a stumbling sinner who really wants to love you. Help me with your powerful graces. Change me from a sinner to a saint.

Spiritual Communion, page 6

Visit With Mary

My gentle Mother, I have disgracefully rebelled against your Son. I am sorry for what I have done. I kneel at your feet, hoping that you will obtain pardon for me. I know you can do so because Saint Bernard calls you the "minister of forgiveness." But I am confident that you will supply me with everything I need: courage to ask forgiveness, perseverance, heaven. I hope to praise your mercy forever, my Queen, for having gained heaven through your ministry.

Concluding Prayer, page 7

TWENTY-THIRD VISIT

Introductory Prayer, page 5

What heavy expense, what dangerous hazards some people willingly face to travel to the Holy Land! They want to visit the places where Christ was born, where he suffered, where he died. We need not travel so far nor face such hazards to be near him. The same Savior lives in the tabernacle of our nearby church. These pilgrims consider it a great privilege to carry away a little dust from the cave where he was born or from the tomb where he was buried. But think of our privilege: not just a remembrance of his life but the reality of his presence!

A holy religious burning with love for the Blessed Sacrament wrote this inspiring letter: "Every good thing that I have comes from the Blessed Sacrament. I have offered myself totally to Jesus in the tabernacle. I can see countless graces left unused in this divine sacrament because souls will not come to ask for them. I can see our Lord's devouring desire to nourish souls from here.

"O wonderful Host in which God's power is so clearly revealed! It embodies everything he has done for us. We need not envy heaven's saints. The God they feast on lives with us too—and with even more marvelous proof of his love! Persuade every soul you can to devote itself to the Blessed Sacrament. I speak like this because this divine bread makes my heart expand with love. I can't stop talking about it. I try to do everything I can for Jesus in the Blessed Sacrament."

Angels in heaven, you adore our God constantly. Fill my

heart with the burning fire of your love. My Jesus, open my eyes so that I can see how astounding is your love for every single human being. The depth of your love should deepen my love. My Lord, I will love you always, and this alone to please you. I believe in you; I trust in you; I love you; I belong to you.

Spiritual Communion, page 6

Visit With Mary

Lovable Lady, Saint Bonaventure called you "the Mother of orphans." The orphans he speaks of are sinners who have lost God their Father. Here is such an orphan. I have lost my Father, but I still have you as my Mother. You can put me back into his good graces. I ask you for help because I know you will listen. No one ever cries out to you without being heard. No one who prays perseveringly to you is ever lost. Only those souls who fail to seek your help eventually find themselves in hell. So if you want me in heaven, my Mother, make me call on you constantly.

Concluding Prayer, page 7

TWENTY-FOURTH VISIT

Introductory Prayer, page 5

You are a hidden God. These words of holy Scripture can be referred to Christ hidden in the Blessed Sacrament. When the Son of God became human, he hid his divinity under humanity. But in this sacrament Christ even hides his humanity. He appears under the form of bread to show how tenderly and warmly he loves us. "The divine is hidden; the human is hidden; love alone is left for all to see," remarks Saint Bernard.

My Redeemer, such lavish love leaves me speechless. To show your love for humanity, you veil majesty, you hide glory, you disguise divine life! In the tabernacle you seem to have only one concern: to prove to souls how much you are interested in them. But do souls thank you in return?

O divine Lover, let me say this: Your intense love for us seems to place our good above your glory. You knew what insults would come your way. You realized that many people would not love you; that many would not believe you are present in this sacrament; that some would crush you under their feet and abuse you in various other ways. Even those who believe in you sometimes offend you with their irreverence in church. Others never come to visit you at all and even neglect to care for the altar on which you live!

If I could only pay with tears—with blood—for the stinging insults your heart receives in this sacrament! I at least resolve to visit you often to prove my love for you.

I hope to make up for some of the ungrateful treatment you suffer in this divine mystery.

O Father in heaven, accept this feeble love of mine in atonement for the insults inflicted on your Son in the Blessed Sacrament. Accept it united to the boundless love that Jesus gave you on the cross and now offers you in this sacrament. My Jesus, I wish I could inspire every human being to love you. Make yourself known and loved!

Spiritual Communion, page 6

Visit With Mary

O powerful Lady, sometimes I get the frightening thought that maybe I will not be saved. Then I turn to you, my Queen, and confidence floods my soul. Why? Because you are so rich in grace! One saint calls you an "ocean of grace." Another says you are a "font of grace." Still another a "fountain of grace and comfort." A fourth says you are "full of goodness." You are so bent on helping souls that you feel hurt if they do not ask you for grace.

O rich, wise, loving Queen, you know better than I do what my soul needs. You love me even more than I love myself. I beg you to obtain for me the graces my soul needs the most. Do this and I will be happy. O God, grant me the graces that Mary asks for me!

Concluding Prayer, page 7

TWENTY-FIFTH VISIT

Introductory Prayer, page 5

Saint Paul praises the unflinching obedience of Christ. *He accepted an obedience,* marvels Paul, *which carried him to death.* But in this sacrament he goes even further. Not only is he obedient to his Father; he is obedient to *humanity!* Not only is he obedient to death; he obeys even until the end of the world.

In obedience to humanity, the King of the universe comes down from heaven! In obedience to humanity, he lives imprisoned on the altar! *I shall not resist.* He allows humans to keep him wherever they wish—in monstrance or tabernacle; to carry him in procession; to bring him into the homes of the sick and dying; to dispense him to all, whether saint or sinner. The gospel tells how marvelously he obeyed Mary and Joseph. Today he obeys every priest in the world. *I shall not resist.*

All the sacraments, O Jesus, and especially this sacrament of the Eucharist, flow forth from your loving heart. I wish I could give you as much honor and glory as you give your Father in this divine mystery. I know you love me now with the same degree of love that compelled you to die on the cross for me. Divine Heart, introduce yourself to those who do not know you. Free the souls in purgatory through the power of your merits. At least ease their suffering, for you are preparing them to become your eternal spouses. I adore you, I thank you, I love you, with every soul who loves you at this moment. Remove from my heart all attachment to worldly things and fill it with your love. Rule it so completely that from now on I can say: *Who will separate me from the love of Christ?*

O divine Heart, engrave on my heart the sufferings you bore so willingly for me. Then when I gaze at them, I will accept and even desire suffering for love of you. Most humble Heart, share your humility with me. O meekest of hearts, make my heart meek like yours. Dismiss from my heart everything you do not like. Direct it toward you so that it will yearn for your will alone. Let me live only to obey you, only to love you, only to please you. I know I have a tremendous debt to pay. And even if I wear myself out in your service, I will hardly have begun to pay it. O Heart of Jesus, you are Lord of my heart.

Spiritual Communion, page 6

Visit With Mary

Saint Bernard speaks of Mary as a "lifeboat." She is a lifeboat that will save us from the shipwreck of eternal damnation. Mary is like the Ark in which Noah escaped the Flood. But she can rescue far more than his Ark did. Only a few people and a few animals were brought to safety in his lifeboat. Mary, our lifeboat, rescues anyone who calls for help. How unfortunate we would be if we did not have Mary! Yet, how many are drowned in hell, my Queen! And why? Because they do not call to you for help. Good Mother, make us always turn to you for help and encouragement.

Concluding Prayer, page 7

TWENTY-SIXTH VISIT

Introductory Prayer, page 5

Sing his praises, O people of God! Great is the Holy One who dwells among you! Imagine! The eternal God is living in our world, in our churches, close to our homes! What joy, what hope, what love, should flood our souls at realizing this tremendous fact! He whose presence is the joy of heaven's saints; he who is love itself living here in the Blessed Sacrament. Saint Bernard said that God does not just *have* love; he *is* love. Then this is not only a sacrament *of* love. It *is* love because it is God. His immense love for souls prompts him to reveal himself as love: "God is love."

But I hear you complain, Lord: *I was a stranger, but you did not welcome me.* You have come into the world to be our guest, and we have refused you hospitality. You are right, Lord. And I am one of those who have left you all alone in an empty church. Reproach me as you please. But I beg you not to punish me as I really deserve—with the loss of your presence. I promise to stop being so rude and selfish. From now on I will visit you often. My Savior, make me faithful to my resolve, and let my example inspire others to visit you. Your Father says that he loves you and is pleased with you. If you can please a perfect God, then certainly an imperfect sinner like myself should find it easy to love you.

O consuming Fire, devour within me every desire for things that distract me from you. You can if you want to: *Lord, if you are willing, you can make me clean.* You have already done so much for me; do this too. Smother every love in my heart that does not lead to you.

I give you my entire self. Starting today I offer every second of my life to the Blessed Sacrament. Be my comfort and my love in life and at death. In those final moments please come and lead me to your kingdom. This is my hope. O my Jesus, when shall I see you face to face?

Spiritual Communion, page 6

Visit With Mary

In you, gentle Mother, we find the cure for all our miseries. You have been called "the strength of our weakness." In you we find release from sin's stubborn grasp. Saint Bonaventure spoke of you as "the gateway to freedom." In you we find peace. He said souls could rest secure in your love. In you we find the answer to all our problems. You have been hailed "our comfort in the pilgrimage of life." In you we find divine grace and God himself. You are "the throne of grace" and "the bridge God uses to communicate with humanity." Our sinfulness has repelled God, but he returns on this wonderful "bridge" to live in our souls. My Mother, you are my strength, my escape, my peace, my hope of salvation!

Concluding Prayer, page 7

TWENTY-SEVENTH VISIT

Introductory Prayer, page 5

"In no other religion throughout the world does God so identify himself with man as he does in ours." The pagans were amazed to hear how much the God of the Christians had done for them. They thought up their gods as they pleased; they could make their gods do anything they wanted them to do. Yet never did they dare invent a god who loved men so extravagantly as our God loves us.

To prove his love and to give grace to his lovers, our God has worked a marvelous miracle. Night and day he remains hidden in a tabernacle—our companion through life. It seems as if he cannot leave us.

My Jesus, you have worked this miracle to satisfy your craving to be near us. Then why do we forget you so often? How can we live apart from you for so long? How can we dare to make our visits so rare? Why does a fifteen-minute visit feel like a century? What tremendous patience you have, my God! I see why: Boundless patience springs from boundless love. It is love that moves you to keep living among such ungrateful people.

Boundless are your perfections, my Lord, and boundless is your love! Never let me appear again in the ranks of the ungrateful. Make me your tireless lover. I used to grow weary in your presence because my love was so weak. But your powerful grace can fan my love into a blazing fire. Then I will never tire of being at your feet.

Eternal Father, I offer you your Son. Accept him from me, and through his merits grant me an active and tender love for the Blessed Sacrament. Draw me like a magnet toward the churches where he is present and make me yearn for my next visit with him. My God, give me an all-embracing love for Jesus in the Eucharist!

Spiritual Communion, page 6

Visit With Mary

Mary is a figure of the tower of David mentioned in the Bible: *A tower with a thousand shields hung upon it.* She is a fortress that can shield all those who run to it for protection. My Lady, one saint called you "a powerful defense for those engaged in battle." My enemies are constantly attacking me. They want to rob me of God's grace and prevent me from seeking your protection. But you are my strength. You take up arms for those who trust in you. That is why Saint Ephrem calls you "a warrior." Defend me, fight for me, my Mother. Your name is my safeguard.

Concluding Prayer, page 7

TWENTY-EIGHTH VISIT

Introductory Prayer, page 5

God the Father has sent his divine Son to redeem us. After such generosity, what can he possibly refuse us, asks Saint Paul. We know, too, that the Father has given his Son everything: *The Father put everything into his hands.* God has made us rich in grace by giving us Christ in the Blessed Sacrament. Let us always thank him for this goodness, this mercy, this overwhelming generosity. *You have become rich through him in every way...now there is no grace that is not yours.*

Savior of the world, you are mine if I say but the word. But can I truthfully say that I am yours—the way you want me to be? Never let me be so ungrateful that I refuse to accept your love: If this has happened in the past, never let it happen again.

Starting today I consecrate myself to you once for all: My life is yours for time and eternity. I offer you in sacrifice my will, my thoughts, my actions, my sufferings. Here I am, Lord—I belong to you. No longer will I cling to earthly things that separate me from you. Inflame my heart with divine love. Make me love others only because I see you in them. You loved me even when I had no love for you. Surely you will accept me now that I consecrate myself to you.

Eternal Father, I offer you the love that animated the heart of Jesus in his life of sanctity. He has applied his divine merits to my sinfulness. Enrich my soul, then, with the graces he asks for me. His merits have brought me countless blessings. With them I pay off the debt of my sins. Through them I expect from you every grace: forgiveness, perseverance, heaven, and especially the soul-changing grace of your love.

It is easy to see that I am the one holding back the flow of grace into my soul. But I trust that you will help me to remove these obstacles. I beg you in the name of Jesus because he has promised: *Whatever you ask the Father in my name, he will give to you.* So, you cannot refuse me. Lord, all I want is to love you—to give myself to you, to stop being so ungrateful to you. This is my prayer. Make today the day of my complete conversion so that I will never stop loving you. I love you, my God, my Love, my Heaven, my Life, my Everything. You hunger for my soul, and I thirst for your love.

Spiritual Communion, page 6

Visit With Mary

You ease my troubles, comfort me in distress, and strengthen me in temptation whenever I call on you, good Mother. The saints were so right when they called you "a port for the troubled," "an aid in distress," "relief for the suffering," and "rest for the restless." Console me, my Mother. I am loaded with sins, surrounded by temptations, cold in my love for God. Please help me to start a new life—a life that will delight both you and your Son. Change me, my Mother; you can do it!

Concluding Prayer, page 7

TWENTY-NINTH VISIT ✓

Introductory Prayer, page 5

I stand at the door and knock. Divine Shepherd, you were not satisfied with sacrificing your life for your sheep. You wanted to remain hidden in this sacrament too. Then, hoping that we would answer, you could knock at the door of our hearts.

I wish I could be near you like the spouse in the Song of Songs who says: *In his shadow I long to rest.* If I really loved you, my Jesus, I would never want to leave your presence. Here, close to your hidden majesty, I would find the soothing rest that your lovers find. Your matchless beauty dazzles me. Your lavish love impels me to say: *Lead me, Lord, wherever you wish.* My only pleasure is to follow you, my Savior.

How well you are pleased, Lord, with virtuous souls who love you in this sacrament. But I blush with shame as I kneel before you. I have no virtues to offer. You ask that your visitors bring gifts: *Do not appear empty-handed before me.* What, then, shall I do? Stop visiting you? No, you wouldn't want that. Despite my poverty, I will come to you knowing that you will give me the gifts I need so much. I realize that you are in this sacrament not only to reward your lovers but also to fill empty souls with your riches.

Start today, my Lord! I adore you as King of my heart. You are a real Lover of souls, a Shepherd who loves his sheep too lavishly. Divine Lover, I approach you today with nothing but a hollow heart. I offer it to you so that loving you will be its only occupation. With this heart I can love you and will love you. Capture it; unite it to your will. Let me be like Saint Paul, who said he was in chains for the sake of your love: *I, Paul, the prisoner of Jesus Christ.* Merge my life with yours, Lord. Teach me to be unselfish—so much so that I would consider myself happy to lose everything, even my life, to be in love with you forever. My Jesus, I love you, I unite myself to you. Let me love you and be united to you always. You alone can satisfy the desires of my heart.

Spiritual Communion, page 6

Visit With Mary

My Queen, a saint once said that you are "the royal road to the Savior." In other words you are the one who guides souls to God. Surely you cannot expect me to draw closer to God if you do not take me by the hand and lead the way. Take hold of me, my Mother. If I resist, use force. Soften my stubborn will with your loving kindness. Pry it loose from worldly things and bring it into harmony with the will of God. Show heaven your power! Show everyone the depth of your mercy! Lead a faithless lover like me back to close union with God. You can make me a saint, my Queen, and I depend on you to do it.

Concluding Prayer, page 7

THIRTIETH VISIT

Introductory Prayer, page 5

Job was terrified when he cried out in despair: *Lord, why do you hide your face?* But when we see Christ hidden in the Blessed Sacrament, we need not tremble. Instead it should inspire us to trust and love him ever more deeply. It is precisely to strengthen our confidence and to prove his love that he hides himself in the tabernacle. He conceals his face to reveal his love. Who would even dare approach him if this divine King were on the altar in the splendor of his majesty? We would be too fearful to confide in him, too afraid to speak of our needs.

What a master stroke of divine genius: Jesus hides under the form of bread so that souls may approach him easily and love him generously. Isaiah was right when he urged his people to let the whole world know the extravagance of your love: *Tell every nation the story of his deeds.*

Divine Heart, you deserve the love of every human heart. O Heart inflamed with love, set me on fire with a new life of love and grace. Bind me to yourself so firmly that I will never again separate myself from you. Heart that shelters souls, accept me! Heart crushed by sin on the cross, make me really sorry for my sins. The burning love you had for me on Calvary has not cooled. You still have an overwhelming desire to unite yourself with me. How can I resist the pressure of your love? By the power of your merits, pierce me with the arrow of your love so that I remain impaled to your heart forever.

I resolve from this moment to please you in every way I can. I will crush human respect and self-indulgence; I will ignore contradictions and renounce all conveniences that keep me from pleasing you perfectly. Lord, give me the courage to love your will. With your overpowering love, smother every other love that is still lingering in my heart.

Spiritual Communion, page 6

Visit With Mary

Saint Bernard tells us that Mary's love for us could not be greater or more powerful. Her love brings us mercy and her power brings us relief. My Queen, you are rich in love and in your power to intercede. You want every soul to be saved. Then I beg you like one of the saints did: "Great Lady, protect me in temptation and strengthen me when I weaken." I struggle daily to escape hell, my Mother. Help me at every moment! But above all, take me by the hand when you see me staggering from weakness. I will have to battle with temptation till the day I die. My Lady, you are my hope, my refuge, my strength; never let me lose the grace of God! In every temptation I resolve to turn to you immediately with this prayer: Mary help me!

Concluding Prayer, page 7

THIRTY-FIRST VISIT

Introductory Prayer, page 5

What a charming scene: Our loving Redeemer sitting at the well waiting for the Samaritan woman. He was worn out from his journey. Yet he was warm and kind to her so that he might touch her soul and change her life.

In much the same way he waits for us in the tabernacle. He invites souls to keep him company so that he might teach them how to love him perfectly. From every altar he seems to be saying: "Souls, why do you stay away? Why do you not come to me? I humble myself like this because I love you. What are you afraid of? I am not here to judge. I hide myself in this sacrament for one purpose: to save everyone who comes to me. *My mission is to save the world, not judge it!*"

Just as Jesus in heaven perpetually pleads our cause, so night and day in this sacrament is he our divine Advocate. He offers himself as a victim to the Father to obtain for us boundless mercy and numerous graces. Thomas á Kempis says that we should speak to Christ in this sacrament without fear, without formality, "as lover to his beloved, as a friend to a friend."

My hidden Lord, with your permission I open my heart to you in full confidence; O divine Lover, I see the sins that many souls commit against you. Your love is not appreciated. You offer them favors; they repay you with insults. You whisper words of love; they scream words of hate. You give them countless graces, but they refuse them. My Jesus, is it really true that I once treated you like that? I'm afraid it is.

I want to change, Lord, and I want to amend my life. For the rest of my days I am determined to do everything I can to please you. Tell me your desires; I want to fulfill them completely. Your wish will be my command. I promise that I will never neglect what I am sure is your will—not even if it means losing relatives, friends, esteem, health, or even life. I am willing to part with everything, so long as it pleases you. Nothing could make me happier than to finally realize that my loss is your gain! I love you, my Lord, because you are more lovable than anything else in the world. And in loving you I unite my poor heart to the rich hearts of the Seraphim, to the heart of Mary, to the heart of Jesus. My God, I love you from the depths of my soul; let it be that way forever. Amen.

Spiritual Communion, page 6

Visit With Mary

A holy man once wrote that our heavenly Queen is forever pleading our cause before the face of God. She is our advocate, because she intercedes for us with her powerful prayers. "She sees our weakness and our dangers," he continued, "and with true mother love she sympathizes with us and helps us."

Look at me, my gentle Mother. Count my present sorrows and heed the future dangers that await me. Pray for me! Pray and never stop praying, I beg of you, until you see me safe in heaven.

Another devout soul writes that, after Jesus, you are the hope of heaven to souls who serve you faithfully. This is the grace I ask for today: let me be your faithful servant till death. Then I will hurry to heaven to adore God forever and to thank you for all eternity.

Concluding Prayer, page 7